THE
LAST CRUSADE

THE
LAST CRUSADE

Previously published as

LIVING IN GOD'S LOVE
The New York Crusade

BILLY GRAHAM

BERKLEY PRAISE, NEW YORK

THE BERKLEY PUBLISHING GROUP
Published by the Penguin Group
Penguin Group (USA) Inc.,
375 Hudson Street, New York, New York 10014, USA
Penguin Group (Canada), 90 Eglinton Avenue East, Suite 700, Toronto, Ontario M4P 2Y3, Canada
(a division of Pearson Penguin Canada Inc.) · Penguin Books Ltd., 80 Strand,
London WC2R 0RL, England · Penguin Group Ireland, 25 St. Stephen's Green, Dublin 2, Ireland
(a division of Penguin Books Ltd.) · Penguin Group (Australia), 250 Camberwell Road,
Camberwell, Victoria 3124, Australia (a division of Pearson Australia Group Pty. Ltd.) · Penguin
Books India Pvt. Ltd., 11 Community Centre, Panchsheel Park, New Delhi—110 017, India ·
Penguin Group (NZ), Cnr. Airborne and Rosedale Roads, Albany, Auckland 1310, New Zealand (a
division of Pearson New Zealand Ltd.) · Penguin Books (South Africa) (Pty.) Ltd., 24 Sturdee
Avenue, Rosebank, Johannesburg 2196, South Africa

Penguin Books Ltd., Registered Offices: 80 Strand, London WC2R 0RL, England

While the author has made every effort to provide accurate telephone numbers and Internet
addresses at the time of publication, neither the publisher nor the author assumes any
responsibility for errors, or for changes that occur after publication. Further, the publisher
does not have any control over and does not assume any responsibility for author or
third-party websites or their content.

Published in association with the literary agency of Alive Communications, Inc.,
7680 Goddard Street, Suite 200, Colorado Springs, Colorado 80920.

All Scripture quotations unless otherwise indicated are taken
from *Holy Bible*: New International Version®. NIV® copyright © 1973,1978,1984, by International
Bible Society. Used by permission of Zondervan Publishing House. All rights reserved.

PRINTING HISTORY
G. P. Putnam's Sons hardcover edition / August 2005
Berkley Praise trade paperback edition / June 2006

Berkley Praise trade paperback ISBN: 0-425-21129-0

The Library of Congress has catalogued the G. P. Putnam's Sons hardcover edition as follows:
Graham, Billy, 1918–
Living in God's love : the New York crusade / Billy Graham.
p.   cm.
ISBN 0-399-15346-2
1. Evangelistic sermons.   2. Baptists—Sermons.   3. Sermons, American—20th century.
I. Title.
BV3797.G67L58   2005   2005052007
252'.06—dc22

PRINTED IN THE UNITED STATES OF AMERICA

10 9 8 7 6 5 4 3 2 1

Contents

THE
LAST CRUSADE

Preface

The volume you hold in your hands represents a living record of the now-historic Billy Graham Crusade in New York City, over three Spirit-filled evenings, June 24, 25, and 26, 2005. The estimated attendance for the three nights was 242,000 people, but as his sermons demonstrate, Billy Graham's message wasn't about how many people attended—it was about reaching each and every person who attended with the Good News that God loves them and can change their lives.

Reading these words from Billy Graham reveals a very important fact: that while the world has changed, his message has stayed the same. Billy Graham began over sixty years ago by preaching the Gospel of Jesus Christ, and now these many years later, it is the Gospel he is still preaching. His gift of making Scripture relevant for each new generation is unequaled, and is one of the many reasons that hundreds of thousands turned out in New York to hear his extraordinary message.

As you read these messages from Billy Graham about God's love, know that he is speaking directly to you, wherever you are, and whoever you are. May his message touch your heart, and bring you comfort and joy.

The publishers wish to express their gratitude to Billy Graham and his staff for their assistance in providing the materials for this book and for editing them for publication.

—The Publishers

Foreword
by Anne Graham Lotz

A Billy Graham Crusade symbolizes and summarizes for me, the second-oldest child of Billy and Ruth Graham, the very ministry that took my father away from our family—for years. Daddy has estimated that he was gone from home approximately sixty percent of the time during his children's growing-up years. But his absences were not those of a normal father who left for work each morning and returned every evening. Daddy was gone for weeks and months at a time.

So you might expect that the last Crusade,

held in June 2005 at Flushing Meadows Corona Park, New York, would bring me some pleasure. Or relief. After all, I adore my father. And now our family gets Daddy back.

But instead of being glad that this was reportedly the last Billy Graham Crusade, I'm fighting tears, wondering . . .

What will it be like for him to never again stand in front of thousands of people and tell them, in his ringing, authoritative voice, that God loves them? What will it be like for him to never again grip the podium in the center of a packed stadium and publicly issue, to each person there, that life-changing invitation to respond to God's love by . . .

. . . placing your faith in Jesus alone,
. . . claiming the Cross as God's sacrifice for your sin,
. . . repenting from sin,

. . . asking Him to forgive you and come into your
   heart,

      . . . surrendering your life to Him as your
      Lord and Savior?

   What will it be like for him to never again hear
the gentle strains of "Just as I Am" echoing above
the quiet shuffle of thousands of feet as people
make their way down stadium steps and cross the
grassy field in order to find God?

   While Daddy's voice may be silent in the sta-
diums and arenas of the world, I am confident that
his message will continue to reverberate throughout the generations to come. My prayer is that
thousands of pastors, teachers, evangelists, and
ordinary men and women will take up the message
like a baton being passed in a relay race and faithfully send it on to those with whom they come in
contact. *Please, dear God, as my father, Your humble
servant, steps down from his life's work, would You*

*Anne Graham Lotz with her father at Flushing Meadows
during the 2005 New York Crusade.*

raise up tens of thousands to take his place? Raise up
an army of men and women who will faithfully com-
municate the message. And Lord, You can begin with
me, because my father's message is Your message.

Daddy's message—God's message—is a message of hope for the future . . .

. . . of love for the present . . .

. . . of forgiveness for the past . . .

It's a message that, when received, brings . . .

. . . a fresh beginning

. . . unshakable joy

. . . unexplainable peace

. . . eternal significance, meaning, and

purpose to life

. . . and opens Heaven's door.

It was this message, which Daddy carried to
the world, that dissolved any potential resentment
in my heart over his absences and created in me a

personal, passionate resolve to communicate it myself to as many people as possible. And so, during the last meeting in Flushing Meadows, as I sat in a folding chair under the broiling sun and listened to Daddy's final Crusade sermon, I silently rededicated my life to picking up and passing on the baton.

So here it is. This is it. The message is timeless . . . the message is truth . . . the message is in this book you now hold in your hand.

Read it . . . then pass it on.

Introduction
by Billy Graham

I love New York, and I always have!

This city has been called "the crossroads of the world"—and with good reason, for no other city on earth is so vibrant, so energetic, and so influential. Over the years I have probably come to New York hundreds of times, and I always feel a thrill of excitement whenever I catch a glimpse of its unforgettable skyline.

New York City has rightly been called a city of neighborhoods, and those neighborhoods are a microcosm of our world—with people from almost every nation, language, ethnic group, and religion imaginable. I have been told that people speaking some 130 languages can be found within walking distance of our meetings in Flushing Meadows Corona Park. Yes, New York City influences the whole world—but the whole world has influenced New York City through the rich diversity of its citizens.

In recent years, however, New York has influenced us in another way: by being a lasting symbol of courage and resiliency in the face of almost overwhelming tragedy. As long as America lasts, the events of September 11, 2001, and following will be indelibly imprinted on our nation's memory. But New York's reaction to what took place on that day will also never fade from our memories. Who can forget the courage of its police and firefighters and other emergency workers during those traumatic days—hundreds of whom paid for their courage with their lives? Volunteers from our own organization came to help feed those who were working at Ground Zero or to assist in other ways, and the stories they told of the unsung sacrifice and heroism they witnessed daily will be with me the rest of my life. And who can forget the determination New Yorkers have shown not only to rebuild, but to make their city even better and more united?

Many people are surprised, however, to learn that in recent years New York has become an influential city in another way—and that is spiritually. Today New York is home not only to many historic churches but also to some of America's most creative and fastest-growing new congregations. Their commitment to their neighborhoods and their involvement in almost every type of social and personal issue could well become a model for America's churches in the future. Some 1,400 churches, representing more than 90 denominations were directly involved in this

2005 Greater New York Crusade, and I commend all those whose vision, hard work, and prayers made this event possible.

Our first Crusade in New York City was in 1957. We were in Madison Square Garden night after night for sixteen weeks, as well as in Yankee Stadium and other venues. It was the longest and most intensive mission we ever held, and it also marked the first time we were on national television on a regular basis. I will never forget the welcome we received then, and the lasting impression this dynamic city and its people made on me. We returned to the tristate area for Crusades several more times, culminating in an unforgettable meeting in Central Park in 1991, with more than a quarter of a million people.

Our three days in Flushing Meadows Corona Park (June 24–26, 2005) marked our eighth—and probably our final—Crusade in the New York area. We will always be grateful to God for the opportunity to meet so many wonderful people and to preach the Gospel during those days. In this book you will read the messages I presented each day. But my prayer is that you won't simply see them as a record of what took place in Corona Park, but that God will use them to speak to your own heart.

Time goes on, our world changes, but Christ never changes, and neither does His power to transform our lives. May you discover this truth through the messages in this book—and may God bless you through them, just as He blessed so many others during the Greater New York Crusade.

—BILLY GRAHAM
June 2005

FRIDAY

June 24, 2005

More than 60,000 people gathered in Flushing Meadows Corona Park on June 24, 2005, for the first night of the Billy Graham Greater New York Crusade. Some 1,400 churches, representing more than 90 denominations, joined in supporting the historic event. At a press conference a few days before, the eighty-six-year-old evangelist acknowledged that it would be his final Crusade in New York, and possibly the last in his long ministry.

Media interest in the event was intense, with reporters coming from around the globe to cover the

Crusade—more than 700 in all. Master of ceremonies for the opening evening was longtime team member Cliff Barrows. The program included greetings from the Crusade's Executive Committee chair, Dr. A. R. Bernard, and a special testimony by Charlotte, North Carolina, businessman Mel Graham, a nephew of Billy Graham. The audience enjoyed music by contemporary Christian artists Salvador and Steven Curtis Chapman. Then longtime team member George Beverly Shea, "America's beloved Gospel singer," gave a memorable rendition of the hymn "The Love of God," singing just before Billy Graham came to speak—as he has done throughout Mr. Graham's ministry.

Billy Graham then welcomed the crowd and spoke from the third chapter of John in the Bible: "You Must Be Born Again." At the conclusion of his message more than 2,200 came forward to indicate their desire to commit their lives to Christ.

WELCOME BY DR. A. R. BERNARD,

CHAIR, THE GREATER NEW YORK CRUSADE,

PASTOR, CHRISTIAN CULTURAL CENTER,

BROOKLYN, NEW YORK

Welcome! Whether you are here on the grounds of Flushing Meadows Park or you're joining us by way of radio, television, or the Internet, welcome. I bid you grace and peace in the name of our Lord and Savior Jesus Christ, to whom be glory and honor and dominion and power forever and ever, amen. Thank God for you and all the prayers that have gone up to make this happen.

Tonight we are a part of history. One of the most respected icons of Christianity in the twentieth century is saying farewell to sixty years of ministry. How will he end? The same way he began, preaching the simple message of God's hope and love for mankind through Jesus Christ.

When CNN reporter Mary Snow asked me what makes Billy Graham loved and respected by so many, my answer was: his integrity and his unwavering commitment to the message of the Gospel. Reaching across denominational, religious, racial, and political lines, he has been able to speak to the culture without compromising his convictions or his representation of the Lord Jesus Christ.

I answered this reporter intuitively at the time, but it was not until I had lunch with Cliff Barrows that I was given the key to the success and longevity of the Graham team. Cliff shared with me that back in 1948, in his hometown of Modesto, California, they decided to covenant together and discover the core values that would drive their evangelism. They said it would be driven by integrity, accountability, purity of lifestyle, and humility. They covenanted together that these four core values would be the driving force behind their personal lives and the life of the Graham organization. They have kept that covenant for more than fifty years—and because of their faithfulness and God's grace, over the next three nights we have the privilege of hearing one of God's generals close out sixty powerful years of evangelical ministry.

What better place to do it than the crossroads of the world, New York City?

It all began in 1957 here, and since then and even since his last visit in 1991, the spiritual landscape of New York City has changed dramatically. No longer is New York City considered to be "the stronghold of Satan," "sin city," or "a city in spiritual darkness." Dr. Graham has returned to a city experiencing radical spiritual transformation. The small storefront churches of our city have grown into twenty-first-century megachurches, with memberships that number in the thousands and tens of thousands. And their members are not content to serve God in the confines of the local church, but are inspired to become points of light within the institutions of government, education, business, and social services. If you don't know it by now, you will know it by Sunday night that God is alive and well in New York City!

Again, I say welcome and God bless you.

"You Must Be Born Again"
by Billy Graham

I thank all of you for being here—not only the people here, but those of you in the other areas of the park watching on the large video screens. Tonight I'd like to say that it's great to be back in New York! Every time I see the slogan that says "I love New York," I always pray for New York, because I love this city. We've been here so many times and stayed so long, and this is a wonderful occasion for me and my associates and my family.

I just had a picture taken with most of my

grandchildren. I didn't know I had that many! I think we have twenty grandchildren and about twenty-five or thirty great-grandchildren, and I think they must all be here.

I'm thankful also for all of our friends that are here. I told the press yesterday that so many old friends were coming that I didn't know whether there would be room for other people! We've had letters and telegrams and e-mails from people all over the country—and all over the world, even— who were coming to these meetings in New York, and I want to welcome all of them, as well as all of you from New York. God bless you all!

With all the kind comments that have been in the paper and on the television in the past few days, I feel a little like I did in Philadelphia many years ago. I was to speak at a conference, and a man got on the elevator and said, "I hear Billy Graham is on this elevator." Dr. Bonnell, who was then pastor of the Fifth Avenue Presbyterian Church in

Billy Graham with some of his grandchildren and great-grandchildren.

Billy Graham surrounded by friends and family.

New York, was with me, and he pointed in my direction and said, "Yes, there he is." This man looked me up and down for about ten seconds, and then he said, "My, what an anticlimax!" After all this music and all that you've read and heard, I'm sure that I'm an anticlimax.

As you've probably read, my sermons are shorter now than they used to be. When we were at Madison Square Garden in 1957, I would preach forty-five minutes, or an hour, or even an hour and a quarter. Today I make them much shorter. I remember many years ago when I preached my first sermon. It was in North Florida in a small place called Bostwick, and a friend of mine had asked me to go with him. He knew I was learning to be a preacher, so he said, "You're going to preach tonight." That night it was cold and they had a big potbellied stove in the middle. He introduced me and I got up to preach, and I had four outlines of sermons that I had prepared to preach somewhere. But that night I preached all four of them in ten minutes!

Tonight I feel just as tense and just as nervous as I did then, because I haven't preached a sermon or given a talk since last September. If you don't use your voice and get used to speaking, it's very difficult to start again—so this is like that first night, because it is the first sermon I've preached in a long time.

I heard about a man years ago who was supposed to speak for twenty minutes, but forty minutes later he was still speaking. So someone threw a gavel at him, but they missed and hit a woman in the front row. She was almost unconscious, but she said, "Hit me again. I can still hear him!" I don't want that to happen tonight!

This is a tremendous place for us to be, here in Flushing Meadows Corona Park, because it was here that the United Nations met for the first five years of its existence. Did you know that? It was also here that the United Nations voted to establish the state of Israel, so Israel was born right here. Today more Jewish people live in New York than in Jerusalem or even in all of Israel.

This is a great and wonderful city, with so many ethnic groups. Yesterday I came here through the park with Art Bailey and Jeff Anderson, who have directed this whole venture. They were showing me the various parts of the park where chairs are being set up, and I ran into groups of people that were praying. There were some Koreans here, and they were praying, and I knew that God was going to mightily bless in answer to prayer.

Now, tonight I want you to turn with me to a passage of Scripture, and I want to talk from that passage. It is found in the third chapter of the Gospel according to John, verses one through seventeen:

Now there was a man of the Pharisees named Nicodemus, a member of the Jewish ruling council. He came to Jesus at night and said, "Rabbi, we know you are a teacher who has come from God. For no one could perform the miraculous signs you are doing if God were not with him."

In reply Jesus declared, "I tell you the truth, no one can see the kingdom of God unless he is born again."

"How can a man be born when he is old?" Nicodemus asked. "Surely he cannot enter a second time into his mother's womb to be born!"

Jesus answered, "I tell you the truth, no one can enter the kingdom of God unless he is born of water and the Spirit. Flesh gives birth to flesh, but the Spirit gives birth to spirit. You should not be surprised at my saying, 'You must be born again.' The wind blows wherever it pleases. You hear its sound, but you cannot tell where it comes from or where it is going. So it is with everyone born of the Spirit."

"How can this be?" Nicodemus asked.

"You are Israel's teacher," said Jesus, "and do you not understand these things? I tell you the truth, we speak of what we know, and we testify to what we have seen, but still you people do not accept our testimony. I have spoken to you of earthly things and you do not believe; how then will you believe if I speak of heavenly things? No one has ever gone into heaven except the one who came from heaven—the Son of Man. Just as Moses lifted up the snake in the desert, so the Son of Man must be lifted up, that everyone who believes in him may have eternal life."

"For God so loved the world that he gave his one and only Son, that whoever believes in him shall not perish but have eternal life. For

God did not send his Son into the world to condemn the world, but to save the world through him."

JOHN 3:1–17

Jesus was preaching and teaching, and the people were following Him and wanted to be near Him, but He would not commit Himself to them. The Bible says, "But Jesus would not entrust Himself to them . . . for He knew what was in a man" (John 2:24–25). He knew that something was wrong with human nature.

Now, there was a man in the crowd by the name of Nicodemus. He was a great teacher, a great professor, a very rich man, and he asked Jesus some spiritual questions. And Jesus said to him, Nicodemus, you're a great man but you lack one thing. You must be born again.

We didn't know what that phrase "born again" meant until Jimmy Carter was elected president and he began to talk about being born again. Then we went through a period that many of you may not remember where there were "born again" automobiles and every other kind of "born again" thing Madison Avenue could think of, using that term.

But Jesus said it is possible to start life all over again, and that's why He said, "You must be born again." Today man's moral ability is lagging behind his technological ability, and it could mean disaster and catastrophe for the whole world. The greatest need in the world today is the transformation of human nature—to make us love instead of hate—and that's what we all need.

I heard about an incident many years ago in the seventh game of the World Series. The score was tied and it was the last inning. The last player came to bat, and he hit a home run out of the park. The crowd went wild! Think of it: It's the last inning of the World Series, with two outs, and you get a home run. But when he came to home plate, the umpire yelled, "Out!" The crowd was stunned. The umpire explained that he hadn't touched first base.

That's the way it is with many of us. We are Christians outwardly; we go to church; we've been baptized or confirmed—but deep inside we need something else. We need to be born again, spiritually reborn, which only Jesus can do for us. He calls on us to repent of our sins and to come to Him by faith.

Don't miss that first base! Nicodemus was a ruler; he was rich; he was religious; he fasted two days a week; he tithed all of his income. He was a professor of theology—but he was not satisfied. There was a void in his life, an emptiness in his heart. Many churches would have been glad to have him as a member, but Jesus said it wasn't enough. "Nicodemus, it is not enough; you must be born again."

Why did Jesus say that? He said it because He

knew what was in man—in our hearts. What causes lying, cheating, racial prejudice? The Bible says that out of the heart come evil thoughts, murders, adulteries, fornication, thefts, false witness, and blasphemies. These are the things that defile a man and defile a country. They defile our world today.

Look at all the things that are happening in our world. Every morning when I have breakfast, I have three newspapers in front of me. One of them is the *New York Times*, and I'm able to see a little of what is happening in our world. Tonight I was interviewed by two of the national television people, and they both asked the same questions: "What's wrong with our world? What's happening? Is there any answer to it?"

The Bible says that our problem is sin. We've broken God's law. We've broken the Ten Commandments. We need to look at the Ten Commandments, because they convict us of our sins. The Bible says if we break God's law in one point, we are guilty of breaking all of it.

The Bible says we are all like sheep—we've gone astray, and we've turned every one to our own way. I remember we used to have some sheep at our place. We bought a place in the mountains of North Carolina years ago for $13 an acre, and we had enough room for some sheep and some goats. I remember a great big red goat came calling on us and took up with us and he had big long horns and we called him "Khrushchev." But we had some sheep also, and the sheep always tried to get out and eat the grass on the other side of the fence.

The Bible says we are like those sheep. We want to get out from the authority of the Ten Commandments. We want to do our own thing, and those things are wrong. We are spiritually dead—dead toward God.

The Scripture says that by one man, sin

entered into the world. That man was Adam, and death came because of his sin. Then death passed upon all men, for all have sinned. We are all sinners, every one of us—and a radical change is needed to find fulfillment in this life, and to be acceptable by God. Nicodemus wasn't satisfied, and he wanted to know why. He wanted to know, What is the new birth? How can a man be born when he's old? He wanted to understand it, but Jesus said it was like the wind, and we can't fully understand it. We can only accept it by faith.

There are many things I don't understand. I turn on the television set in my hotel room here and watch color television. I don't understand anything about it, except I understand the switch—that's all. I can't fix things; I've never been able to fix things at home that needed fixing. I don't understand a computer. I don't understand the Internet. There are so many new technologies that I don't understand, and I was told by a top technological expert a few weeks ago that what we have today is only the beginning of what is going to happen in the next five or ten years.

How do we go about proving a mother's love? You love your mother, but how do you prove it? Can you do it in a laboratory? No. There are some things we just don't understand.

The Bible says all our righteousness is like filthy rags in the sight of God. All the good works that we do don't count anything toward Heaven. After you receive Christ, you want to do all the good works you can, but before that, you must repent and come to Christ by faith. When Jesus came, He didn't come just to teach us how to live. He came to die on the cross.

Many of you saw the film *The Passion of the Christ* that Mel Gibson put out. Some liked it and some didn't, but when the Pope saw it, he said, "That's the way it was." There was a lot of violence when Roman soldiers scourged someone. They were scourged for nine minutes, and those steel pellets on the end of the scourge cut to the very bone.

Jesus endured all that, and then they took Him outside of Jerusalem and put Him on a cross. Crucifixion was the most terrible death you can imagine, but that wasn't the worst suffering Jesus endured. The real suffering was when He said, "My God, why have you forsaken me?" In that terrible moment, God the Father turned His back on His Son, because His Son was bearing the sin of the whole world—every sin that has ever been committed, every sin that you have ever done, every sin that I've ever committed. On that cross He bore our sins and shed His blood for us. He took the punishment we deserve.

I heard about a couple in Oklahoma recently. They went to the city to see *The Phantom of the Opera* but it was sold out and they couldn't get a ticket. So as people came out after the show, the couple picked up some of the discarded programs and ticket stubs, and they would sing one of the songs, but they never actually got to see the show. When they went back home, however, they told everybody how wonderful it was. They could show the tickets, they could sing the songs, but they hadn't actually seen it. That's the way it is with many of us tonight. We have all the trappings of true faith, but deep inside, we've never been born again.

One time, when I was in Poland, when it was a Communist-controlled country, we had been invited by the Catholic and Protestant churches to preach in a number of cities. In Warsaw they gave a dinner for us at the beginning of our trip, and I sat beside a Roman Catholic monsignor. He said, "You know, I got my Ph.D. at the University of Chicago." He spoke perfect English. He added, "One day I was on a bus and a woman was sitting behind me, a black woman, and she looked at me and said, 'Have you ever been born again?' I told her that I was a clergyman, a father in the church, and had a theological education. And she said, 'That's not the question I asked you. I asked you, have you ever been born again?'" And he said he got back to his room in Chicago and he said he began to think about it. "I took down my Bible and some other things I had, and I saw where Jesus said to Nicodemus that you must be born again. I got down on my knees and I prayed that God would forgive me and come into my life. My life totally changed." He added, "I don't know whether that was the new birth, or a renewal of my Confirmation vows, or exactly what it was, but something happened to me that was very similar to what Jesus told Nicodemus, and my life has never been the same."

You have been born into a human family, but when you are born again, you are born into God's family. I'm asking you tonight to come and be born into God's family. What is it? The Bible says we receive the word of God, being "born again, not of perishable seed, but of the imperishable, through the living and enduring word of God" (1 Peter 1:23). Then when you come to Christ, He comes to live in your heart. The Bible says you become the temple of God, because the Spirit of God dwells in you. Tonight I know the Holy Spirit lives within me, and He lives within hundreds of you.

Since I've been in New York, there have been two helicopter crashes in the East River. I was reminded of a man who was on a small plane going from Nassau to Miami. It crashed in the ocean. He survived the crash, but had blood on his forehead which attracted the sharks, and he spent ten hours kicking at the sharks to survive. After he had been in the water more than ten hours, he saw an aircraft and waved his orange life vest. The pilot spotted him and dropped a smoke canister and radioed a Coast Guard cutter that was twelve minutes away. He said, "Hurry! There's a man down there surrounded by sharks." So the Coast Guard went there and found him and saved him. You know, he didn't need a new swimming technique, he needed outside intervention.

And tonight, you need outside intervention—and that's what God will do for you. He'll bring a peace and a joy to your heart that you've never known. He'll fill the void that's in your heart. Some of you here tonight have been looking for something for years. Others of you are young. But no matter who you are, you are searching for peace and meaning and a purpose in life. What do you have to do? By faith open your heart to Christ and say, "Lord Jesus, come into my heart"—and He will.

I'm going to ask you to do that, as we've seen thousands of people do all over the world. I'm going to ask you to get up out of your seat and come and stand in front here, and before you go back, I'll say a word to you and have a prayer with you. In the other areas of this park, where the large screens are, you can come forward also. When you come, there will be counselors that have been trained to help you and answer your questions. Come now and give your life to Christ.

God Bless You.

Following the invitation for people to commit their lives to Christ, Billy Graham then spoke to those who had come forward.

Now I want to say a word to all of you who have come forward. You have come tonight not to Billy Graham, not to Dr. Bernard, not to Cliff Barrows or anyone like that. You have come instead to Jesus; you have come to the cross. Can you imagine when He went to the cross, what He suffered for you? He came to die for us. And tonight you have come to say, "Lord, thank you for dying for me. I open my heart to You. I'm willing to turn from my sins and change my life, but You're going to have to help me. I can't change it myself. You'll have to help." When you sincerely say that, He will send the Holy Spirit to help you change. Then, by faith, receive Him into your life as your Lord and Savior. When you go home, read the little book that we are going to give you tonight, which has part of the Bible in it. It's important to read the Scriptures, and even if you don't understand it all, it will speak to you. We're going to give you the Gospel according to John that we used tonight.

Now I want you to pray a prayer after me, out loud, right now: "Oh God, I am a sinner. I am sorry for my sin. I now turn to Jesus for forgiveness, and I thank You for what You have done for me through Him. I receive Jesus into my heart, and I want Him to be the Lord of my life. I want to follow Him in the fellowship of His Church. Take charge of me, Lord. Help me in my problems. Lift the burdens of my heart. Make a new person out of me. In Jesus' name, we pray. Amen."

SATURDAY

June 25, 2005

Saturday evening, June 25, was Youth Night at the Billy Graham Greater New York Crusade in Flushing Meadows Corona Park, with more than 80,000 people filling the chairs in the main park and spilling into the overflow areas to watch the event on huge television screens.

Youth nights at Billy Graham Crusades have always been special, with lots of lively contemporary Christian music and other highlights geared toward the younger generation. Saturday's Crusade events actually began with some 12,000 children gathering for Kidz Gig, a lively presentation of the Gospel in song and drama featuring Bibleman. At the end of the unusual event, hundreds indicated a desire to commit their lives to Christ.

Saturday evening brought together some of contemporary Christian music's best-known artists, including Jars of Clay, Nicole C. Mullen, and Tree 63. Special platform guests included former president Bill Clinton and New York Mayor Michael R. Bloomberg (both of whom spoke briefly to the audience), and New York senators Charles Schumer and Hillary Rodham Clinton.

Billy Graham's Youth Night message was titled "The Rich Young Ruler," based on Mark 10:17–27. By the end of the evening more than 4,200 people had registered their decision for Christ that day, either at the Kidz Gig in the morning or at the evening service.

GREETING BY

FRANKLIN GRAHAM,

SON OF EVANGELIST BILLY GRAHAM

Good evening. I am Franklin Graham, and I want to welcome all of you tonight. I came to New York when I was thirteen years old to go to high school out here at Stony Brook on Long Island. New York was a great experience for me, and I came to love this state, especially New York City.

But when I came to New York, even though I was raised in the home of an evangelist preacher, I didn't want God in my life. The last thing I wanted was God telling me what to do. I wanted to party, I wanted to have fun, I wanted to enjoy life—just like a lot of you who want to experience life to the fullest. Well, I did, and yet there was something missing in my life.

Then I left New York and went on to college. During those years I wanted to live for Franklin Graham; I didn't want to live for the Lord Jesus Christ. It wasn't that I didn't believe in God; I did believe in God. There are millions of people in this country that believe in God. But I didn't want God to be the center of my life. I didn't want His Son to be on the throne of my life. I believed in God, but I didn't want His authority in my life. And yet, I can't explain it, but there was an emptiness in the life of Franklin Graham, and the more I tried to have fun—the more I tried to experience the things that life had to offer—the emptier I became.

There may be some of you here tonight who have that same emptiness in your life. You have a big black empty hole in your life, and you've tried

Billy Graham's son, Franklin, giving his testimony.

to fill it with drugs, with sex or alcohol, or maybe you've been thinking, "If I can just make a lot of money, that will make me happy. I'll find the dream of my life."

Well, I can tell you, none of these things will satisfy. Yes, you may have fun for a while. I did, but then I'd have to wake up in the morning and realize that there was an emptiness in my life that nothing could fill. So one night I got down on my knees and said, "God, I have sinned against You. I am sorry. I need your forgiveness, and I need Jesus Christ to come into my heart and into my life to take control."

You see, the Bible says we have all sinned; we all have come short of God's glory, and the wages of sin is death. But God still loves us. The Bible says that God so loved the world that He gave us His only begotten Son, that whoever believes in Him will not perish but have everlasting life.

I was twenty-two years old when I got on my

knees, asked God to forgive me, and asked Jesus Christ to come into my heart and my life. That night, God forgave Franklin Graham—not because I am the son of Billy Graham, not because of who my parents were.

You see, I went to church. I was religious, but religion cannot save you. My father preached last night on Nicodemus, who was a religious man, but Jesus said, Nicodemus, it's not enough. You've got to be born again. And I'm here to tell you today, you must be born again. If you are here tonight and you don't know Jesus Christ as your personal Lord and Savior, tonight you can experience the forgiveness of sin. God will forgive you of every sin you've ever committed. God will give you a new life, a new beginning—but you must come to God His way.

Jesus said, "I am the way and the truth and the life. No one comes to the Father except through me" (John 14:6). Tonight you are going to have an opportunity in a few moments, when my father comes, to put your faith and trust in the Son of God, the Lord Jesus Christ.

If you're here tonight and you've never had your sins forgiven, if you're not sure where you're going to spend eternity, you can be sure tonight. When my father gives that invitation in a few minutes, get up out of your seat and make your way to the front, or if you're in one of the overflow areas, make your way to one of the screens, and say Yes to the Lord Jesus Christ. Invite Him to come into your heart and life. He will change you, He will cleanse you, and you will have a new life and a new beginning. He did it for me, and if He'll forgive Franklin Graham, He'll forgive you.

But it's a choice you must make. You have to invite Him to come into your heart, to come into your life. No one else can invite Christ into your life. You have to do it yourself. Will you do that tonight? God bless you.

The Rich Young Ruler

by Billy Graham

onight I want to talk to you about a young man that came to Jesus many years ago. You can read about him in Mark 10:17–27.

As Jesus started on his way, a man ran up to him and fell on his knees before him. "Good teacher," he asked, "what must I do to inherit eternal life?"

"Why do you call me good?" Jesus answered. "No one is good—except God alone. You know the commandments: 'Do not murder, do not commit adultery, do not steal, do not give false testimony, do not defraud, honor your father and mother.'"

"Teacher," he declared, "all these I have kept since I was a boy."

Jesus looked at him and loved him. "One thing you lack," he said. "Go, sell everything you have and give it to the poor, and you will have treasure in heaven. Then come, follow me."

At this the man's face fell. He went away sad, because he had great wealth.

Jesus looked around and said to his disciples, "How hard it is for the rich to enter the kingdom of God!"

The disciples were amazed at his words. But Jesus said again, "Children, how hard it is to enter the kingdom of God! It is easier for a camel to go through the eye of a needle than for a rich man to enter the kingdom of God."

The disciples were even more amazed, and said to each other, "Who then can be saved?"

Jesus looked at them and said, "With man this is impossible, but not with God; all things are possible with God."

MARK 10:17–27

I heard about a man in California, a drunken cowboy who came out of a saloon. He had a six-gun, and he was shooting at the legs of people and they were dancing all around. An old man came on his donkey from the mountains, and the cowboy said, "Old man, have you ever danced?" And the old man said, "No, I haven't." And the cowboy said, "You're going to learn." And he began to shoot at the old man's feet, and the old man did dance around. A little bit later, the old mountaineer reached into his saddlebag and pulled out a sawed-off shotgun and said, "Young man, have you ever kissed a donkey?" And the cowboy looked at that gun and said, "No, but I've always wanted to!"

I've always wanted to come back to New York. This is our second night, and last night we had a wonderful night back here. It's great to be back.

I read the other day a discouraging article about the singer Madonna. She was being interviewed, and she said, and I quote her, "You read about wars, and you read about the senseless killings and the famines and the AIDS epidemic, and you think, *Where is it all going? Why am I here? What do I believe in? What's the whole of life? Is there life beyond this world that we live in?*" Some of you here tonight are asking the same questions. What is life all about? Where did you come from? Why are you here? And where are you going?

In the March 14, 2005, issue of *Time*, the cover

had a haunting black-and-white photograph of a desperate and nearly lifeless-looking woman. You may remember it. The mother had three children clinging to her, and the headline said, "How to end poverty." Millions die each year because they are too poor to live. One of my friends wrote after seeing the article, "It grips my heart, and I'll think, *how can this be, in a world with so much wealth?*" But this is our reality. We live on a ravaged planet, affected by sin in every part: the earth, the sky, the sea, the animals, and especially the human family.

In Genesis, the Bible tells us that God made us in His image. We were meant to be like God! But sin intervened. We rebelled against God, and now there is another kind of poverty that plagues us—a poverty of the soul, where our longings are never satisfied, where our desires are never filled, where our hopes are unrealized and fears grow.

Some of you tonight are in that situation. You

Franklin escorts his father to the podium.

have a girlfriend or a boyfriend who has left you, or you might have a death in your family, or you may have a habit that you cannot control. You have tried to control it, but you've failed.

The Bible says God has put eternity in our hearts. We long to know God, and to know exactly what life is all about. Every day we strive to change our surroundings for the better, thinking that will make us happy, or we live in denial. But this is an inescapable Biblical truth: We were made by God to be better, and to have a better world.

Some time ago, Bono of U2 came to see us at our home, and he sat in front of my wife and composed a song. He was there about three or four hours, and we had a wonderful time with him. In one of his songs he says that we are "stranded in some skin and bones." Saint Augustine, the great Christian, wrote almost sixteen hundred years ago, "Our hearts are restless until they find their rest in thee." Those words are true. At the end of the millennium, MTV counted down the top rock songs of all time. Do you know what the number-one song was? "Satisfaction," by the Rolling Stones. Its opening lines became the anthem of many youth today: "I can't get no satisfaction, 'cause I try and I try and I try and I try."

Jesus, however, says our hearts can be satisfied. He said, "Come to me, all you who are weary and burdened, and I will give you rest. Take my yoke upon you and learn from me, for I am gentle and humble in heart, and you will find rest for your souls" (Matthew 11:28–29). Come to Jesus tonight and let Him control your life and forgive your sins. Let Him give you assurance that if you died tonight, you would go to Heaven. He will change your life and take away your emptiness.

In the new *Star Wars* movie we see a young man who made a wrong decision about his life. His inner desire to control events and to play God led to his destruction. The decisions you make tonight will affect your whole future—your future in this life and your eternal future. Where you are in a thousand years will depend, to a large extent, on what you decide tonight. This young man who came to Jesus was searching. He was looking for the most important thing in life, and he was missing it. He needed God at the center of his life.

I read somewhere that what young people want and need from older people first of all is to be loved. You want to be loved, and the Bible says God loves you. God loves *you*! God loves everyone here tonight. Then young people want to be recognized as individuals, and they want to be trusted. Older people need to recognize the need a young person has for privacy. Young people also want to be accepted. To a young person, total rejection is almost a living Hell. They want to be respected and listened to. Young people also want their parents to forgive them—just as sometimes they need to forgive their parents. They want the security and the authority of discipline, and they want discipline to be modeled in the way their parents live, as well as in what they say. Above all, they want something or someone to believe in. They want to believe in something that satisfies their heart and gives them assurance for the future.

Many of you have just gotten out of high school; some of you are going to attend a college or university. Perhaps you're just out of school and looking forward to enjoying the summer and maybe starting a new job. But in your mind, there's something you still haven't found: You haven't found purpose, you haven't found meaning. You can only find it in God, who created you.

Look at all the stars you see in the sky. We are in the galaxy we call the Milky Way, and I've been told there are 200 billion stars in our Milky Way. But there are millions and millions more galaxies in the universe—and God made them all. He is that great! It's beyond our ability to understand.

The Bible says that God has no beginning, He has no end. Our minds cannot comprehend that; it's beyond us. But we aren't like God. We will all die. War does not increase death. Did you ever think about that? We're all under the sentence of death. We're all going to die—and we all need to be ready to meet God.

How do you do that? How can you be ready to meet God? That's the reason Jesus Christ came. He came to die on a cross, and when He died on that cross, He said, "My God, my God, why have you forsaken me?" (Mark 15:34). In that moment, God had laid on Him the sins of all of us—your sins and my sins and everyone's sins. And we're forgiven by God, because of what Jesus did on the cross.

But He didn't stay on the cross. He was buried—and then He rose again. God raised Him from the dead, and today He is alive! Jesus said, "I am the way and the truth and the life" (John 14:6). And then He added an interesting statement: "No one comes to the Father except through me." The way to God is through Jesus, for only He died and rose again to take away our sins. The Bible says, "Neither is there salvation in any other: for there is none other name under heaven given among men whereby we must be saved" (Acts 4:12, KJV).

You know, Buddha said at the end of his life, "I'm still searching for truth." Jesus said "I am the truth." He said "I am the life." He could say that for one reason: He is God in human form. The proof is His resurrection from the dead.

Some of you are looking for satisfaction chemically, in drugs or alcohol. It's not there. You've already discovered that by seeing other people that are broken down and have ruined their lives. We see a lot of publicity today about binge drinking. Perhaps you have a good time for a few minutes, a few hours, then it all comes to destruction and you're still searching. Or emotionally, you try to find an answer in sex, and it's not there. Oh yes,

there is pleasure in sex. Sex was given to us by God, and there is no sin in sex unless you are not living according to the Word of God. But you'll not find the meaning of life in sex. There is an emptiness and loneliness after it's all over.

Perhaps these same things were in the heart and mind of this young man. He came to Jesus and he fell down before Jesus, and he asked, "What do I have to do to inherit eternal life?" He asked the right question. He did the right thing, by coming to Jesus. He came at the right time, when he was young. He came with the right attitude, in humility. He got the right answer, to come and follow Jesus. But he did the wrong thing: he turned away. The Scripture says that Jesus loved him. And Jesus loves you tonight, no matter what is wrong in your life, and He can change your life.

One observer wrote some time ago that "if there is a theme running through rock music at the beginning of the twenty-first century, it is a pervasive sense of hurt. If this era's music says anything, it is that a generation sees itself as uniquely fractured." Perhaps that is the way you feel.

If you are here tonight hurting, feeling the pain of abandonment and rejection, I want you to know that your Heavenly Father has not abandoned you, and never will. A friend wrote that when she received Christ, "All my life built up to that one moment when I ran out of myself and God took me over."

Tonight I'm going to ask you in the various parts of this park to get up out of your seat and come to Christ. Come down here and stand, or stand in front of the screen if you are in one of the side areas. After you have come, I'm going to say a word to you, have a prayer with you, and then we will give you some literature that you can take home to help you in your new Christian life. You may be a church member. Last night I heard that we had two pastors that came forward, and there are others here tonight who go to church—but that's not enough. You need Jesus. He wants to come into your heart, and you can find Him tonight. If you need a language other than English, you'll see signs for your language group, and you can go there and find some people who will talk to you and pray with you.

*Billy Graham at the press conference prior to the launch
of the historic 2005 New York Crusade.*

Following his message, Billy Graham spoke to those who came forward at his invitation to commit their lives to Christ.

Now, for all of you that have come, I want you to pray together a prayer with me out loud: "O God, I am a sinner. I am sorry for my sin. I am willing to turn from my sin and I want to receive Jesus as my Savior. I want to confess Him as Lord. From tonight on, I want to follow Him and serve Him in the fellowship of His Church. In Jesus' name, Amen."

Now, if you sincerely prayed that prayer, you have made your commitment to Christ, and God heard you. He sees your heart and He knows what you meant.

From tonight on, there are four things that are very important that I want you to remember. You're going to get them in some literature we are going to give you.

First of all, read your Bible every day. That helps you to grow. "Desire the sincere milk of the word, that ye may grow thereby" the Scripture says (1 Peter 2:2, KJV).

Then the second thing is to pray. You may say, "I don't know how to pray." There's a simple prayer that I pray many times a day: I say, "Lord help me." We all have our problems. We all have our difficulties, we all have our challenges, and we can say, "Lord, help me in Jesus' name." Just talk to the Lord like you're talking to a friend.

Then the third thing is to go to church. Be sure

you get into a church where Christ is proclaimed. I'm not telling you which denomination to join or which church, but I hope you'll be faithful in going to church.

Then fourth, witness for Christ by your words, and the smile on your face, when you are at work or school, or by going out of your way to befriend a person in need, or of another race or background. Go out of your way to be their friend and show them Christ's love. Some of you who live here in New York or other parts of the country have neighbors that you have never met. Go out of your way to go and say, "I went to the Crusade and Christ touched my life, and I want to be your friend." Help them to know that you have been changed and you are different, because of Christ. The same can happen to them, and God wants you to touch their lives.

God bless you.

SUNDAY

June 26, 2005

The final day of the 2005 Billy Graham Greater New York Crusade turned out to be one of the hottest of the summer, but the heat and humidity couldn't dampen the enthusiasm and interest of the estimated 90,000 who gathered for the evangelist's final message.

A stellar list of Christian musicians called the audience's attention to Christ's power to change lives, and included Ricky Skaggs, Marcos Witt, the Gaither Vocal Band, MercyMe, and Michael W. Smith. A deeply moving video also was shown honoring those who lost their lives in the World Trade Center terrorist attack on September 11, 2001, and prayer was offered for all who had been afflicted by that tragic event.

A special guest appearance by the famous Brooklyn Tabernacle Choir added to the event's worshipful atmosphere, and ninety-six-year-old George Beverly Shea sang one of the world's best-loved Gospel hymns, "How Great Thou Art," just before Billy Graham came to the podium to preach. Basing his message on the theme of Noah and the Second Coming of Christ, Billy Graham spoke freely not only about his own mortality, but also of the fact that every human being faces death. At the conclusion of the service, almost 3,000 came forward at the evangelist's invitation to express their desire to follow Christ.

In all, almost a quarter of a million people attended the Billy Graham Greater New York Crusade, with more than 9,400 registering a commitment to follow Christ. The meetings were also broadcast live over a special network of radio stations across the country.

"This may be the end of the Crusade meetings," Mr. Graham said later, "but for many in New York it is only a beginning—the beginning of a new life in Christ. For that we praise God, and we will continue to pray for this city and its people."

When Christ Comes Again

by Billy Graham

I t's hard for me to believe that this is Sunday—toward the end of our three days in New York. We hope to come back again someday. I was asked in an interview if this was our last Crusade, and I said it probably is in New York. But I also said, "I never say never." And the man who was interviewing me agreed that "never" is a bad word because we never know what the future holds. We think we can predict it, but then things turn out much differently.

That happened to a man I heard about some years ago. He came to New York from Texas, and he went to see the horses race at Belmont and he really enjoyed himself. Since he was a Baptist from Texas, he wasn't supposed to gamble. But then he saw an interesting thing: he saw a Catholic priest blessing a horse, and that horse won—and that happened three times. So he said to himself, "This isn't gambling; this is a sure thing!" When he saw the priest blessing another horse, he put all the money he had on that horse.

The horse started out around the track, and about halfway he began to buck and foam at the mouth, and he fell over dead. So the Texan went over to the priest and said, "What happened? You blessed three horses and they won, but the fourth horse fell over dead." The priest looked at him and said, "You must not be a Catholic." And he said, "No, I'm a Baptist." Then the priest said to him, "If you had been a Catholic, you would have known

the difference between a blessing and the Last Rites!" By the way, I told that story when I was here in 1957, before most of you were born.

Now, tonight I want to thank some of those people I missed thanking last night. I want to thank Mayor Bloomberg for coming last night. I also neglected to thank Senator Schumer, who was here all evening, and I appreciate it. And I want to thank the committee that invited us here: Dr. Bernard and Dr. Johansen, and the ministers I've talked to since I've been here, the executive committee of pastors and laymen who worked together. I also want to thank Art Bailey, who was the director of these meetings, and also Jeff Anderson, who set this whole thing up. Whoever dreamed of turning Corona Park into something like this? Jeff Anderson and his staff did this. And I want to thank the press, the newspapers, magazines, radio, and television, for all that they have done. In fact, it's the most media attention I've ever seen in this city concerning evangelism, and I'm deeply grateful to them. But especially I want to thank my longtime friends and associates who have put up with me for so many years—over sixty years we've been together: Cliff Barrows and George Beverly Shea. They are two of the greatest men of God I have ever known.

Sitting up here on the platform is a longtime friend, Richard Bewes, who has been a minister for many years of a great Anglican church in London, and we're going to talk about going to London, possibly, for a Crusade. We love London, and we have held many Crusades in Great Britain. But most of all I want to thank all the people who have prayed and worked for these meetings, and there's no way to express my gratitude. Thank you, and may God bless you for all you have done.

Tonight I want to talk to you about a man that you've all heard about. His name was Noah. Have you ever heard of Noah and the flood? I heard about a man in Pennsylvania who survived the Johnstown flood that killed so many people, and afterward, he spent his life going around giving talks about the Johnstown flood, and he loved to do that. Well, when he got to Heaven, Peter asked him what he would like to do in Heaven. He said, "I'd like to give a speech on the Johnstown flood." And Peter said, "That would be fine, you can do that, but remember that Noah is in the audience!"

Tonight I want to talk about the flood that came in Noah's day, and what the Bible says about the days that are coming, in the future. This is what Jesus said about the end of the world, and the days before He comes again:

No one knows about that day or hour, not even the angels in heaven, nor the Son, but only the Father. As it was in the days of Noah, so it will be at the coming of the Son of Man. For in the days before the flood, people were

eating and drinking, marrying and giving in marriage, up to the day Noah entered the ark; and they knew nothing about what would happen until the flood came and took them all away. That is how it will be at the coming of the Son of Man.

MATTHEW 24:36–39

Almost everyone today understands that we are approaching a climactic moment in history. There is going to come a time when the world will end—not the earth—but the world system in which we live, which the Bible calls "Of Satan." In the New Testament, the "new birth" is mentioned nine times. Repentance is mentioned about seventy times. Baptism is mentioned some twenty times. But the coming again of Christ is mentioned hundreds of times.

Jesus Christ said, As the days of Noah were, so shall also the coming of the Son of Man be

(Matthew 24:37). When the situation in the world becomes like it was in Noah's day, you can look up and know that Jesus is coming soon. In Noah's day, the world was filled with wickedness, corruption, violence; every imagination of man's thought was evil. It was a world in which marriage was abused. It was a world in which violence prevailed. Think of the headlines in our papers today. The world is headed in the same direction.

Noah's world was also a world of decadent religion. Today many people are religious. In fact, religion is one of the great things in America today. The mayor of New York and I were talking about it last night, and he said, "This is a very religious city." And he's right, this is a religious city. There are many religions here. Almost every religion you can think of in the whole world is represented in New York. But in Noah's time religion had grown corrupt and decadent, and the same thing could happen

today. Jesus said that in the latter days many false prophets would arise.

Today I believe God is warning us. I think of the disappearance of that beautiful girl in Aruba. I think of those three little children that were smothered to death in the trunk of an automobile. I think of all the evil things that we read about every day. But Noah was a good man. He walked with God, the Bible says. He was beloved by God. He was a man of moral integrity. He worshipped God, and we need to worship God today with prayer and Bible study.

The Bible says, "By faith Noah, when warned about things not yet seen, in holy fear built an ark to save his family" (Hebrews 11:7). Think of that: he was moved with fear. Is it legitimate for a person to come to Christ out of fear? Absolutely. Many people in the Bible came to God out of fear.

But also, God is a God of love. The primary thing about Jesus in the New Testament is that He loves you. Some of you feel unloved. Some of you feel depressed, or you feel you don't have purpose and meaning in your life. He is there to rescue you from that situation that you're in, and He will forgive all your sins, because when He died on the cross, God laid on Him the sins of all of us. It would be great if you could go home tonight and know that all the past is different, that you are different, that you have a new relationship with God by faith.

The Bible says that Noah was terrified. He was not only afraid, he was terrified, and God told him to go build a ship. Now, you think of it: In the middle of the desert, he is told to build a ship 450 feet long, 45 feet high, with one window and one side door.

During that whole time, Noah was preaching to the people: repent, repent, repent! That was the first sermon John the Baptist ever preached; that was the first sermon Jesus ever preached: "Repent, for the kingdom of God is at hand." Noah was scoffed at, of course. People laughed at him and probably threw rocks at him, because it took a hundred and twenty years to build that ship.

I recently read an article by Rabbi James Rudin, speculating what it would have been like if there had been 24-hour-a-day television in Noah's time. Think of CNN and Fox and MSNBC and all of those shows that go night and day. Suppose they had been around in Noah's day? Naturally, such a large shipbuilding project would have attracted media attention.

Noah would have been pressed to explain his mysterious actions. They wouldn't have understood it. Then his family would have been scoffed at for the grim prediction that a flood was going to come, and the weather service would have been certain that no rainstorm could possibly last forty days and forty nights.

But the destructive flood eventually came.

One hundred and twenty years had passed when God came to Noah one day and said, "Noah, it's going to start raining in seven days. You have seven days to bring your family and all the animals in." Noah didn't have to beat the bushes to get the animals in. They came because God inspired them to come into the ark. The people kept scoffing—but suddenly it was too late.

The only bright spot I see on the horizon today, when I read the press, is the coming again of Christ. I believe He is coming back. In the New Testament, there are so many passages on the coming again of Christ that I could spend all afternoon reading them. "I go to prepare a place for you," said Jesus. "And if I go and prepare a place for you, I will come again, and receive you unto myself; that where I am, there ye may be also" (John 14:2–3, KJV).

If I died right now, I'd go straight into Heaven and see Jesus. Most of the interviews I've had here in New York have talked about death. Just a few minutes ago I was talking to television journalist Chris Matthews and he asked the same question about death: "What happens when you die? Are you looking forward to death?" "Yes, I'm looking forward to death," I told him.

Yes, we're going to die. We're all under judgment. War does not increase death. Did you know that? You think about that. There were thousands of people killed when we invaded Europe in 1945 at Normandy, and there are thousands of people that have died in Iraq and Vietnam and Korea and many other places, but that does not increase the rate of death, because we are all going to die. But at death we are going to be divided: Some will be eternally lost, and some will be eternally saved. We are saved through Jesus if we put our faith in Him, because Jesus went to prepare a place for us, and He loves us.

When Christ was ascending into Heaven, fol-

lowing His death and resurrection, the angels asked His disciples, "Why do you stand here looking into the sky? This same Jesus, who has been taken up into heaven from you will come back in the same way you have seen him go into heaven" (Acts 1:11). Jesus is going to come back. Are you ready?

When is that going to happen? When the disciples met together, they asked Him, "Lord, are You at this time going to restore the Kingdom?" He said to them, "It is not for you to know the times or dates the Father has set by his own authority" (Acts 1:6–7). Jesus also said that no one knows that day or hour, not even the angels, but My Father only knows the date that I'm coming back (Matthew 24:36). But the Scripture says, "For the Lord himself shall descend from Heaven with a shout, with the voice of the archangel, and with the trump of God: and the dead in Christ shall rise" (I Thessalonians 4:16, KJV). There is going to come a day when you will hear a gigantic noise from Heaven—a shout—then the archangel is going to speak. And at that moment, those that have died—your fathers, your mothers, your relatives, your friends that are dead in Christ—are going to rise from the dead.

For years every time I came to New York through LaGuardia Airport, I would pass a graveyard on the way down to Times Square. I don't know what the name of it is, but there are graveyards all over New York, and those graves are going to be opened if they are people who knew Christ as their Lord and Savior. And those who are left here that are still living are going to join them. Where? In the air—on our way to Heaven.

And then, the Bible teaches, there is going to be a great coronation. Millions of angels, along with millions of people who have followed Christ in their life here on this earth, are going to have a gigantic banquet called "the marriage supper of the Lamb." Jesus is the Lamb, and He is going to be crowned King of kings and Lord of lords.

What a glorious moment that's going to be! I'm looking forward to that. In fact, George Beverly Shea, whom you just heard sing so beautifully "How Great Thou Art," is ninety-six. I'm eighty-six, on my way to eighty-seven. I know that it won't be long before both of us are going to be in Heaven.

Jesus said, "Be ready." In Amos, the fourth chapter, it says, "Prepare to meet your God." Are you prepared? Have you opened your heart to Jesus? Have you repented of your sins?

You say, "What is repentance?" Repentance means you say to God, "I am a sinner. I am sorry for my sins, I'm willing to turn from my sins, but Lord, You have to help me to turn. I've tried so many times to give up things I know are wrong, but I just can't do it. I need Your help. Then by faith, you receive Jesus who died on the cross for you. You open your heart and say, "Yes, Lord Jesus, come in. I'm ready to follow You."

I recently received a letter from someone who said their daughter had suddenly become very ill with an incurable disease, and they were devastated. The letter continued, "Until that moment, I had been bulldozing my way through life. Caught up in driving ambition, in a business where everything had to be done yesterday. I was successful. I was so busy that I lost all my spirituality. I never thought about God. I had forgotten how to pray."

Does that sound like you? There are many people in the New York area that could identify with that mother. You've come to this Crusade expecting to live many more years, but you don't know.

This might be the last day of your life. We never know. The Bible says that "Today is the accepted time, today is the day of salvation!" The Scripture says, quoting God, "I will not always strive with man." There comes a time when it is too late. The only way you can come to Christ is with the Holy Spirit helping you to come—and He will help you, but not always.

There comes a time when it will be too late for you. I'm going to ask you to come to Christ *today*. This may be the last opportunity you will ever have.

I'm going to ask you to get up out of your seat and come in front of this platform and say tonight, "I want Jesus in my heart. And I'm going to do my best to repent of my sins and follow Him."

And if you are watching in some of the other parts of the stadium, you can come to the front of that television screen and there will be people there to talk with you and pray with you and give you some literature to help you in your Christian life. I'm going to ask you to come now and receive Christ into your heart.

God bless you.

A Final Word from Billy Graham

My team and I will never forget those remarkable three days in Flushing Meadows Corona Park. God truly answered the prayers of His people—not just by bringing overflow crowds to the meetings each day, but also by changing countless individual lives through the power of the Gospel. Our world is constantly changing—New York is constantly changing—but the needs of our hearts remain the same, and so does God's power to transform our lives and give us hope for the future. Thousands discovered this truth during those days in New York.

This can be your discovery as well. Perhaps you find yourself confused and puzzled, wondering if there is any meaning or purpose to life. Perhaps you have become captive to some habit or lifestyle that you know could destroy you—and yet you can't seem to do anything about it. Perhaps your life is filled with fear or guilt or anxiety or disappointment, or you are living with wrong decisions from the past that constantly haunt you.

No matter what your problem is, if you and I could sit down and talk I would want to tell you one great truth: God loves you, and He can make a difference in your life if you will let Him. God loves you so much that He sent His Son into the world to die for your sins. When we open our hearts to Christ, He forgives our sins and comes to live within us by His Holy Spirit. He also gives us strength for the present and hope for the future. This is the message of the Gospel—and this is the message you have read in this book.

I invite you to surrender your life to Jesus Christ, and to know the peace He alone can bring—peace with God, peace in your heart, and peace with those around you. By a simple prayer of faith, you can make your commitment to Him today, just as we saw thousands do each day at Corona Park. Don't delay, but by faith ask Him to come into your life to save you and change you—and He will.

God Bless You

Billy Graham

For further information, contact

The Billy Graham Evangelistic Association

1 Billy Graham Parkway

Charlotte, NC 28201

or www.billygraham.org